# BALANCING DISCIPLINE AND LOVE IN PARENTING AND EDUCATION

# BALANCING DISCIPLINE AND LOVE IN PARENTING AND EDUCATION

AVERY NIGHTINGALE

Creative Quill Press

# CONTENTS

# CHAPTER 1

# Introduction

We parents in the United States disproportionately value nurturing behaviors, as well as our relationships with our children, compared with the parents in other parts of the world. In direct contrast, parents hailing from cultures that stress the interdependence of human beings, compared with those of European-American backgrounds, stress the necessity of respect and observation in parenting education. The regard for discipline in those cultures is often at odds with what creating nurturing spaces in U.S. homes may take, and educating children may be of a different flavor elsewhere.

In the U.S. as well, educators seem under pressure to discount the role of discipline in activity creation. Where we generally assume teachers are in the classroom to "teach kids and amplify learning," across the state, school boards, administrators, and educational leaders make it clear that creating classroom spaces of deep learning and discipline is undesirable because those spaces need only to be nurturing (we seem to treat education and discipline as oxymoronic). Thus, "balancing" discipline and nurturing is certainly a fraught enterprise on both home and school fronts; discipline in our cultures may often end up being indistinguishable from abuse (we get especially squeamish when we think discipline and love are competing) and may not make much sense in constellations with education, let alone nurturing, whether we are educators or at home dealing with teenagers. Two questions undergird the work here. Can we balance or use discipline and nurturing in both homes and classrooms? If we can, as there is at least some hesitancy to do so in each set of educational spaces, what is lost for ourselves and young people in denying them education, discipline, and ultimately nurturing home spaces, classrooms, and schools?

# CHAPTER 2

# The Importance of Discipline

Discipline can mold a child into a great personality. Discipline can be compared to a machine, as any device requires the right input, and when the output is not expected, the machine needs to be opened and parts examined. President Abdul Kalam, in his book 'Ignited Minds', says, "It has been my personal experience that the educators who are concerned with preserving Indian culture and ensuring its overall development have widely used the strong foundation of family values, placed discipline over prestige, loved the teaching profession as a divine call, modeled as idealized teaching, cultivated habits of industry and perseverance, inculcated faith in the country and the society, and continually inspired the young minds. I can confidently say that the quality of teachers and their commitment has a direct bearing on producing ignited minds who consequently would be the leaders of character."

I have observed with great wonder an incident that took place in 1965. An elephant calf, just about six months old, arrived at the Mysore zoo and was given to the keepers of the elephants to rear the calf. The experienced keeper, Amma, came into the scene, took the calf, and gave it a sound slap. As it was in an unfamiliar environment, the calf was upset and very much disturbed. Then it was tied to a tree at a safe distance from the herd of elephants. After seeing the disciplined nature of the elephants, the calf did become a happy member of the herd. I used to feed the calf when Amma used to be away from the zoo premises. I visited the zoo just a year back (i.e. nearly 40 years after the event that took place), and the same calf was present at the spot where I used to feed. On seeing me after 40 years, the animal tried to come close to me. The same respect to the people who fed remained with that animal for over 40 years.

Discipline is very important in every individual, irrespective of gender, age, and social status, whether the individual is a child or an adult. Discipline needs to be practiced from the early years of childhood. The great Greek philosopher gave prime importance to the discipline of a child, as he believed that the future of a child depends on the way he or she is brought up by the people who look after him or her.

# CHAPTER 3

# The Power of Love

In writing about these aspects, which result (as we have said) from our task with children — greater whole and "participating in himself by participating in the environment as to it's said — we did not intend to come up with a new definition of life and existence. Instead, we wanted to bear witness, to some extent, with new forms and new words as to our taught public. By adding the love we owe to life and established relationships to Stokes' concern about the need for following the track, beyond the frontiers of inspiration, into the most hidden recesses of the soul that observes the Moon, we are leaving a little alcove where we used to close ourselves off every time the desire passed by on the threshold of love. We kiss it, and then, hand in hand, we go towards the Moon.

Having taken a look at the resources made available to us by Positive Discipline and Montessori, we can feel more confident about the contributions made to education, and, for that matter, to the family, faculties all the way from infancy. We are actually speaking the language of love. We use the courage-filled action that is faith in mankind, in the education and cooperation made real in every child's conquest of himself, and prepared for the future. An education in this spirit offers discipline in activity, freedom in the relationship with adults and with the other children, an invitation to always become increasingly human in the fullness of values.

# CHAPTER 4

# Finding the Right Balance

In this paper, I argue that, given the lack of research concerning the training's capacity to induce nonabusive forms of discipline, the Netting Container (and likely other primary prevention training for parents and teachers in the field) is not sufficient to reach its goal. On the whole, the latter can be harmful, as parents might consider themselves to be well-prepared to raise their children and to know how to avoid abusive parenting. Consequently, parents, when raising their children, might not seek further information or intervention. Given the fact that abusive discipline is still widely prevalent in society, a broader scale specifically regarding abuse as distinct from nonabusive discipline that aims to not only reduce abuse but also to stimulate nonabusive discipline is urgently needed.

Consortium researchers, clinical child psychologists Elizabeth T. Gershoff and Anne E. Rodeheffer, and their colleagues claim to have achieved the Hong Kong police force when rates of physical and psychological violence against kids lowered after the training. As argued by the United Nations (1989) and consistent with the research conducted, they touch on appropriate means of discipline that do not include corporal punishment. Although their critique does not address the larger question of whether the HKPF has achieved their broader goal of using nonabusive discipline, their scrutiny of the Netting Container's efficacy is valid. With these two studies in mind, the task of educating adults regarding nonabusive punishment and improving the Netting Container as a training tool is a vital first step.

# CHAPTER 5

# Strategies for Balancing Discipline and Love

The first step toward the construction of a discipline system that will balance boundaries and love is to decide with your loved ones the kind of discipline that must be used in your house. This can be agreed upon by the parents or guardians, but also by whoever is close during the most significant times of the child's life. Once the decision has been made on the main discipline style to be used in the home, everyone who has to face the child in decision-making situations must adopt and be consistent using the agreed-upon system to maintain the future discipline system of the child. When the same kind of discipline is used by various people, it is less likely that we will be heard as "good" or "benevolent" by the children, but we will be given greater legitimacy as leaders, since it will be clear that we all speak the same language in disciplinary matters.

First, we need to listen to our own inner voice. If we do not exercise the self-discipline necessary to educate our children and guarantee they receive the love they need to feel supported, nobody else will do it for us. We should also remember that we only have to control our reactions one minute at a time. If we keep asking how to act instead of letting our feelings control us, our hearts will tend to be more loving and we will be able to nourish the child who has come to us to learn from us. The child growing up next to us is not interested in metaphysical discussions about love; the one who longs for what we have to teach is waiting to receive it from us. If he sees that we build with love and correct with discipline, he will surely learn to build constructively and correct the results of his mistakes.

How can we find the balance of love and discipline that is so necessary in each child's life without going to one extreme or the other? Here are a few strategies that can be helpful:

*5.1. Setting Clear Expectations*

A first step to reduce children's misbehaviors is much simpler than we imagine, which is to warn them in a pleasant and assertive way what is expected of them, to remind them whenever possible that others can also be offended, and that they must change their behavior. Our idea of what is acceptable varies greatly from human to human, so we must always be empathetic and demonstrate love whenever we ask our children or our students to change their attitudes. Discipline and love should not be opposite poles. After all, how can children develop respect for the rules and for adults, if they perceive that we only focus on their attitudes when they are wrong?

It can be (and frequently is) hard work to set clear expectations for our kids. Sometimes, we don't even realize our expectations are unclear until our kids fail (we're all imperfect). But one of the least loving and most unfair things we can do is to not communicate our expectations clearly. For example, you would insist on your workplace delivering specific guidelines to your job roles, so that later on, your boss doesn't criticize your work: the rule also applies to your kids. As adults, we need to do the same for our kids. They need it both at home and at school, since the family and school roles are not separate, but complementary.

### 5.2. Using Positive Reinforcement

Children seem to be physically, psychologically, and emotionally decomposing in the absence of positive reinforcement. Children vary according to the strength of their positive reinforcement, which allows them to make demands and do what they have done according to the value of the reward they will receive. As a result, children are forced to make decisions not according to what they think is right but according to the value of what they will receive and to shape their behaviors according to their parents' expectations and desires, not the children's own desires, needs, and the situation they have lived. For this reason, the most important property and value is for parents to educate their children to have emotionally dominant children. All of the tasks that will reveal the children's feelings and desires should be done by them.

In positive reinforcement, the subject continues the expressed desires and behaviors, just as it continues to receive gifts, bribes, rewards, praise, encouragement, and praise. In negative reinforcement, the subject recovers from the feeling and behavior when it feels natural, through feedback, scolding, reproach, beating, throwing stones, or something bad and bitter is felt as soon as it is.

The third pair of components of structured democratic parenting, where the parents are exclusively or predominantly dominant, is positive reinforcement and its opposite, negative reinforcement. Positive reinforcement is like praise, encouragement, a bribe, or a gift given for expressing a desire and behavior for something good. Negative reinforcement is like punishment, scolding, or reprimand instead of doing something or feeling something bad and bad for something bad.

*5.3. Providing Consistent Boundaries*

It is important for children to feel loved, valued, and regarded. Hence, parents must be warm, kind, and stroke their children, but they need consistent boundaries and being allowed to clearly understand the educative objectives they set. Children need to be loved with discipline and disciplined without missing love. "The welcoming embrace of the good mother and the demanding look of the good father," as an ancient statesman affirmed. Very often, the balance between nurturing and limits lies in the experience of the single family, generations, and cultures, which are irreplaceable resources for parents in need of understanding the growth needs of their proteges or the inability to meet them. In our society, which is so harmful for the educative reason, the support and encouragement of teachers are even more critical because mothers and fathers are usually on their own in this complex commitment, the education.

As a teacher, Illyene was particularly astonished by parents who invested an enormous amount of time discussing the education of their children with teachers, helping them with individual problems, and then, all of a sudden, principal-centered, rigid, and demanding patients. It is a typical example of bi-disciplinary attitude. Instead, an authoritarian model based on a challenge-centered education, which is particularly perilous in the permissive environment of the last few decades and has been imposed by parents trying, too late, to make up for their educative omissions or lack of interest. Too often focused on physical aspect and outward achievements, these parents are, deep down, disoriented, uncertain, and anxious. They do not stand it when their children express their doubts or vulnerabilities. This is why they expect too much from school, which must ensure, as stated in the Senate Hall, even "the development of character."

### 5.4. Practicing Active Listening

Through practices such as meditation and active listening, which help us in training in non-violent communication or empathic communication, for just to mention two very powerful, very effective tools for humanizing our relationships and influence, we can become these educators who inspire more by the social interest they develop in the subjects that he captivates and respects, with whom they communicate. To clarify a little more what this word seems to want to say, empathy is the ability we develop to put ourselves in the place of the other, perceive and understand all the feelings involved at a particular time in the communication or interaction with the group.

While trying to avoid falling into the trap of trying to be an assertive parent, I have observed that my biggest challenges came from the stormy relationship that we experienced with ourselves, with our emotional states of anguish, fear, frustration, guilt, anger, disappointment, around our habitual need to control, judge, impose, demand respect and attention and to know everything, whenever we are accompanied by someone smaller and dependent on us, namely, being a parent around children or being an educational professional around our students.

In addition to learning to relax and meditate, being an excellent observer of our emotional reactions and being objective to the point of sharing with someone whom you expose to our reactions are essential attitudes to prevent our child from reliving the traumas that our emotional mismanagement may provoke or our moralizing educational rigidity, which become rituals of anger and indignation, often transforming gestation into a martyrdom of depression or rebellion.

*5.5. Encouraging Independence*

The restrictions in this case are heavy, the abuse sometimes produces negative effects. With abusive restrictions and severity we can cause a conflict with the child, apathy, which will accentuate disobedience. In the educational process it is necessary for the child to maturely assume the way he thinks. Children must be taught to act. Children need to make a plan, to act consciously, to know that their thoughts are correct, that the well-being of others, the kindness, the charity make way for a beautiful and harmonious development of the personality, for a good relationship with all the people.

To be more controlled, we generally try to manage them too much - to eat a lot of food, to wash properly, to insist on health, to control every step, to be afraid of getting dirty and damaging clothes, to anticipate any danger. We want to protect them, to help them, but we are not aware of the harm to them, the blocking of the children's independence. Helping, protecting directly arouses the child's lack of self-esteem, the thought that he will achieve less without help. With this help we only achieve the maintenance of our antiquated intervention, we do not allow any reflection and initiative to come from the child.

# CHAPTER 6

# The Role of Communication

As a human creation, communication is linked to love, which is superior to all phenomena, to all the manifestations of the human being along his/her entire life: birth, childhood, adolescence, maturity, old age. Love can be defined as an affective attitude, of affinity, of sharing, respect, protection, moral, durable, stable. This phenomenon opens to personal efforts and implies honoring the other as an individual, of letting him or her be free and knowing how to win the other's trust at the same time. Love activates its own moral from the interpersonal standpoint, for it develops: kindness, tolerance, and availability; admiration and respect; common affective feelings between the person who loves and whom he/she loves. The complexity of the phenomenon permits the complexity of love to be perfectly appreciated by its identification, the affective and emotional implications, the moral, the intellectual, and the artistic ones. Given these considerations, love needs communication to express itself.

Communication is an active and sharing process. It starts from the principle that each individual is unique and special and gets involved with his/her presence, thoughts, experiences, emotions, initiative, authenticity. When we communicate, we come in contact with the other who reveals him/herself through his/her own world, we commune with the other – we join in assisting the forming and complete realization of the being. At the theoretical level, mastering the communication process means knowledge of the general directions of the interpersonal relationship in functions of: personality, non-verbal communication, the communication act, the credit for the dialogue partner, the degree of empathy, the options to continue the dialogue as interpersonal dynamics, personal behavior flexibility, the personality of the dialogue partner and their optimizing elements. The process of communication cannot be reduced to a series of individual behavioral acts through which people transfer the information, but is an extensive, complex process, connected to the whole personality and the experience of the interlocutors involved.

# CHAPTER 7

# Understanding Developmental Stages

Our goal is to help our child meet each new stage in his or her life with the best possible attitude and the least possible frustration. The task, however, becomes difficult and very relative, because the various stages of your child's development will differ from what's considered normal. As such, it becomes essential to determine the developmental problems that can arise during childhood, since they can be detected, referred for treatment, or even eliminated. Frequent doctor visits in the first few years of life can help detect developmental problems and prevent some of these problems from becoming serious. Moreover, it provides an opportunity to collaborate with professionals and fine-tune a set of family-centered goals that are mutually agreed upon and suitable for achieving a better outcome. An essential aspect to remember when dealing with a developmental problem is that even when unavoidable intervention is required, this does not mean our child would not continue to grow into a considered normal member of society.

We need to understand child development from infancy through adolescence. A natural part of what is called "maturation," child development unfolds in various stages, with each stage characterized by a number of important changes. Realizing, for example, that most two-year-olds are trying to separate from protective adults and become more independent allows us to accept with greater patience a behavior that is not always convenient. Understanding that most 3 to 7-year-olds have a vivid imagination and often confuse reality with fantasy will prompt us to be more imaginative in our explanations and less critical of lies, fibs, and stealing from our child's "make-believe" money jar. Knowing that most adolescents are trying to understand their rapidly changing bodies and are often insecure about themselves will make us more accepting of their exhibit of one extreme or another.

# CHAPTER 8

# Adjusting Strategies for Different Ages

Primary school: After the second year of primary school, the children should be mature and cooperative enough for reason to be a more effective educational tool. It is easy to be understood, since it is closer to their way of thinking than simple pictures that make their world more secure to them. The advantage of reason is that once explained to the children, a given cultural standard is enforced by the moral authorities as the standard to be followed in a fair social life. When it is self-stimulated reasoning instead that comes into play, we get what people call consciousness, and it is a source of solid virtues, such as honesty, loyalty, honoring a promise, and many others. High up cultures reach maturity late; those of classical antiquity or from the Far East also required the notion of reincarnation to give a real sense to this kind of education.

Young children: Firm discipline is essential for children under the age of five. The Dalai Lama was right when he said that for the first few years of life, what a child needs most is the mother's love, as almost everything the child experiences during this period shapes the child's mental life from deep within, beyond conscious recall, and influences all subsequent personal and social experiences. However, are those two incompatible requirements, discipline and loving presence, ever interrelated then? This is an important question because secure love is also what a child needs most for a sound psychic development, and love has many tentacles that can be used to direct and retrieve the child, letting it explore safely within the boundaries so set.

# CHAPTER 9

# Overcoming Challenges

Patience can even be seen as a basic key to open the understanding of individuals who play the role of responsible ones for the construction of these citizens. Hence, the search for loneliness in the face of emotions that can even cause shocks to the beliefs inherent in this child is not the answer, but the agony that makes these relationships so rich and persuasive.

Overcoming these difficulties is a huge challenge for parents and educators, but this task, like all educational procedures, is based on reflection and on collaborative common looking. This dialogue does not need to be exhausted, but we propose the search for alternatives in the construction of this dialogical process, which eliminates the dual "I-You" relationship and creates a process of unity, building a strong "Us". It is wonderful to recognize society as a school, both in the formal processes of the school system and in the informal processes, which also belong to everyone's daily lives.

Gradually, factors such as work, lack of time and rest have been negatively impacting those responsible for the education of these children, since they are unable (in the most common situations) to attend to their educational needs, which are expressed in the construction of dialogue and the belief in their children.

Despite its advantages, the use of positive discipline faces one major criticism, which is that it is often considered expensive, that is, requiring much energy, time, and patience to practice it. It is hard to find educators and parents who feel encouraged to respect their children's choices, who are in fact exercising the liberating process of freedom. Although the benefits can be substantial, especially in terms of long-term child behavior, this is an issue that still needs to be addressed.

### 9.1. Dealing with Tantrums

Eliza, who is now 3½, is more mystified than frustrated because she is inching up the walls of Step One School. She knows better than to clip or unclip her chair at the dining table, to pull the table-cloth or to engage her sister in their bedroom. She sees and remembers the consequence of her actions. Now, neither Mrs. Maysam nor Marwa's attitude changed since the marble incident concerning Marwa, nor did Marwa become smarter in the meantime. The treatment Eliza receives seems to be an effective form of discipline, for it succeeds in instructing her in the art of self-control. It's actually fair to illustrate 'how a stone can kill two birds.' There are actually three lessons in one. The youngest sister is being trained to cope with items in its control. Assistant teachers take the children out for controlled trips. The best-behaved are selected on the basis of their behavior en route, and one of the reasons Eliza so adores the bouncing castle and sandpit in the pre-school is that it's proof she is considered mature for her age.

Four-year-old Marwa picks up a marble and walks away with it. Her mother, Mrs. Hani, quickly catches up with her, tells her to give it back, threatening a spanking. Marwa throws herself on the ground and starts shouting her head off. Relieved of her tears, she looks around to see if anybody's noticed her tantrum. Seeing her mother's back, she starts screaming in intervals. Mrs. Hani continues her shopping undisturbed. When they get home, her daughter shows no remorse for her unparalleled performance that Mrs. Hani only half watched. Marwa was a merry child all evening. Mrs. Hani loves her girls unconditionally. Their needs are a priority in her life. Although flexible, there is discipline in her endless devotion. She doesn't believe in chastisement as a form of discipline.

### 9.2. Handling Peer Pressure

The boy becomes a true human only after he reaches the age of a teenager. Until then, he lives simply because it becomes easy for him to contact his friends, his playmates who always move with him. Before his teenage years, the misunderstandings which arise between classmates become matured with certain principles and their school fades away. Here, he is able to create a clear relationship with any or both the brothers and sisters. Hence, the safeguard of the friends can be clearly given to bring up the children. The bonds of friendships become stronger when the friends approach to console the children in the hard times. They protect the secret of the child and move so closely with the child in his hard times. More than friends who move closely in hard times, the children would be attached to the friends who used to react joyfully to the child's joyful movements. The friends who react to the sorrows in the same way the child reacts would lessen the psychological depressions of the child and the child starts accepting their emotional response as love and starts living freely.

Many children are addicted to the habit of chain smoking when they are influenced by peer pressure in colleges. When a new boy contacts with those who are already addicted to smoking and if he unwillingly accepts to smoke under pressure, he gets habituated to this. It is also true that teenagers seek friendships when they are affected by their raging hormones. They should be guided properly about friendship on the right path. It is also true that no parents allow their wards to learn bad things. It is true that even after repeated advice, if the children continue their bad habits, set them to counseling. The children would change definitely after counseling if the counseling has taken place to create change in the children. Do not be remorseful too much for your ward's behavior. Because, the children's character decides as to how they behave with strangers and friends. Some of the brothers encourage the friendship of their sister's son because they live separately with their sister's family and once in a while they meet their sister also.

Everywhere, the student or child is affected by peer pressure. The children are introduced to peer pressure much before their parents are aware of it. Especially when the child is admitted as a new boy in a school, the child faces peer pressure. If he is shy in nature and if he is not able to adjust with the classmates easily, he feels isolated. His classmates start asking him whether he was not allowed to learn in a school from his parents, taken out from nature, etc. It causes the child to feel an inferiority complex in his mind.

### 9.3. Addressing Academic Pressure

The mother then opened her heart... after her child's birth, serious complications had characterized the beginning of their life-long medical journey. In taking him to school, the very idea that he may need a different environment terrified her, reminding her of the worst time of sibling-exclusion and parental judgment where they have experienced ignorance and abandonment from community, families, circles, and close friends. The words of the principal followed the mother's poignant revelation. This time of school success over this time of healing... of mental health first, last and foremost until adolescence, they have only one opportunity to get stronger, more secure, with positive self-esteem whether they have challenges or are our top achievers, we want our students to feel that their special pyrotechnic magic is accomplished and appreciated."

Specialized in children's and young people's mental health, Elizabeth Letarte, president and founder of the Un Monde Par Tous Foundation, and a member of our association, works tirelessly to help combat the psychological distress that can arise from the hyper-competitiveness of our school systems, chanting "ut unum sint," oneness of heart, with all her psychological, medical, therapeutic, and educational soul. "A few days ago," she wrote, "a mother brought her 5-year-old child to my office for a difficult kindergarten transition in a public school... tears, tantrums, and desperate morning threes were becoming a terrible reality for this family. And as the preschool teacher registered the family's pain and escalating struggle, she contacted the principal for an intervention in collaboration with the child psychiatrist and psychologist. On a meeting, the school personnel informed the mother that her child should indeed be equitably accommodated until school entry if a developmental and clinical report requested varied accommodations: less overstimulation, more predictable daily routine, break space to regulate emotions. All measures that they proposed without modification requested by the mother that she needed to understand in order to consent."

### 9.4. Managing Technology Use

Knowing that excessive use and easy access to non-educational internet use becomes associated with greater educational technology, parents had to set guidelines for electronics based on personal consumption, school and domestic environment. Interviewees consistently banned video games during the week at their home, as well as other activities with electronics, such as downloading files from the internet and chatting online. The father of Sara A said, "Sara's friends can chat daily, but will do it in moderation because they are close to their families. If they spend too much time chatting, Zila [her friend's mother] will call the girls to do another activity." Safe-guarding time with friends and family during the kids' week, the deliberate scheduling of activities, and control of social interaction in digital media were recognized as decisive by many of the inter-viewed parents. Heading to the non-access policy for games and other activities directly supervised by parents, the maintenance of a closed domestic encounter was scored by these guardians as key deciding factors for restraint and friendly technology usage.

While a few firms like Google and Apple have been concerned enough about their responsibilities that they have limited their own employees' use of technology, the vast majority of corporations have not yet taken any active steps to help consumers control their use of the many potentially addictive, attention-grabbing aspects of their products, and many corporations regularly engineer their products to exploit vulnerabilities in human psychology so as to maximize the amount of time that their technologically-mediated revenue streams continue. The bottom line is that there is no inherent trade-off between finding a solution to the drowning of otherwise develop-mentally normal children in a technology tsunami, and nurturing technologically well-evolved (though probably not evolutionarily or ecologically justifiable) Pavlovian consumers. That is, in principle, we can nurture our human technical-technological partnership with wisdom and kindness, in part by developing social standards and legal restrictions that support well-informed citizens to use our technology wisely, and in part by keeping our scientifically informed education and parenting focused on nourishing the positive aspects of the human technical-technological symbiosis, while minimizing the negative aspects.

*9.5. Navigating Cultural Differences*

Backing and Hersey (2000) noted that nearly 90% of respondents from a largely White group of parents agreed that parents should spank their children who misbehave, and near 70% believed that such methods do not seriously harm children. In contrast, only 70% of African American respondents agreed that children who do not do well in school should be publicly humiliated and that spanking is an effective discipline method. Instead, more than 80% of African American respondents agreed that parents should make sure that children who do not help around the house do not enjoy weekend fun activities. In another study, Edwards (2007) found that, after an exciting event, moral disapproval, followed by verbal and corporal punishment, was rated in the order of importance by parents from low-income families.

Morality, as composed by spanking, yelling, and love withdrawal, is derived from family myths and then instituted by families and their domains; however, morality is distributed to cultures within these families. Multiculturalism has become an underrepresented theme in research, and assumptions have abounded regarding parent-child discipline, which have proven to be empirically false (e.g., conservative self-righteousness, demanded child independence and responsibility). Over the last 30 years, there has been an increase in racioethnic-nonspecific categorizations of constructs, such as discipline, and despite slight gains in bias-free classifying, multiracial sampling is still at a disadvantage. This is important, as it introduces problems with validity and theory explanation, as construct validity is weakened with population heterogeneity.

# CHAPTER 10

# Seeking Support and Resources

Adults also have some current support in this work. Some find that reading literature, learning skills from courses, or speaking with others of the same beliefs supports them. Recent studies found postpartum mothers experience a decrease in anger when they dedicated more time to adult administration. Asking for help in contexts that make you angry or circulating among those who share your beliefs about parenting can be beneficial. Those that do not have a sympathetic community may want to debate matters more joyfully among other partners, friends, and society members who expect self-control from adults significantly.

Most of the decisions to discipline are learned through trial and error. If you think you need help, seek out your spouse or partner, friends, family members, or even your child's doctor. Ask them what they think about various guidelines/advice you may have come across: "Does this make sense?" and "Is that consistent with joy? How would I do this specific thing?" Before you find out the principle to impose a new method, it can help to imagine what it would look like to perform that method in practice. Be specific: "How often would I make that method for my 4-year-old?" or "What else could I do, instead of shouting, to make sure he will do his job?" When considering varying approaches from others, think about translating each of them into actions.

# CHAPTER 11

# Conclusion

Japan's more successful educational curricula is based on learning morals and values through different school subjects. Love is an inherent part of transmitting these values and disciplining students. Indeed, to discipline without love is to manipulate and a parent or teacher should never do what is not loving according to Kojin Wada, SJ. Often, to discipline is much more demanding and difficult task than to love. Nevertheless, a parent and teacher need to accomplish the task for the sake of the goodness of the children. To teach children to discipline themselves against their excessive desires, to teach children to submit themselves to something greater than themselves, and to provide children with opportunities and time to face uncertainties are highly demanding acts of love on the part of parents and educators to foster and further develop the ethical goodness of children. The same is also true in film art. We need to recover the harmony of discipline and love that we all possess in youth and reform what we have inherited where we have lost the harmony.

The challenge for those in the field of parenting and education is to find the balance between warmth and discipline. In recent decades, some child-rearing specialists have practiced the permissive style of upbringing that facilitates warmth but tends to lessen discipline. They have thought that discipline would make their children less spontaneous and turn them into products of manipulation and less capable of achieving self-direction and self-regulation. Their concern arose from the goodness that they want their children to possess. Takanobu Otomo, SJ believed that the golden mean between being strict and being facile in upbringing is discipline.